The Great Communicator

The Great Communicator

by

with an introduction by **Susan Stamberg**

COLLOQUIAL BOOKS

Published by

COLLOQUIAL BOOKS
Cincinnati, Ohio

Copyright© 1985 by Jim Borgman
All Rights Reserved

Library of Congress Catalogue Card Number **85-72732**
ISBN **0-9609632-1-9**

The contents of this book originally appeared in the *Cincinnati Enquirer,* ©1982, 1983, 1984, 1985. Most of the cartoons which appear here in color originally appeared in color in the Sunday *Cincinnati Enquirer.*
Jim Borgman's cartoons are distributed exclusively by *King Features Syndicate.*

Printing by *Central Printing*
Typography by *Deerfield Press*

For Mary Jo, Kathy and Tom

Special Thanks to:

    Greg Gruenwald

    Polly Burnell

    Marian Borgman

    Gary Watson

    George Blake

    Thom Gephardt

    Bill Keating

    Fran Price

    Mark Mikolajczyk

    The Engraving Department of *The Cincinnati Enquirer*

INTRODUCTION

I'm trying to remember when I first realized that some of what we said each evening on National Public Radio's *All Things Considered* ended up as black marks on Jim Borgman's drawing board. Probably it was during NPR's 3,787th financial crisis. Or maybe the 3,786th.

Yes, it *was* the 3,786th, because that was when Borgman phoned to ask whether he could donate one of his cartoons to us to offer as a premium to listeners we were urging to help solve our crisis.

For crisis #3,787, he published a cartoon about us in which I'm depicted talking into a microphone while my partner, Noah Adams, works the treadmill that powers the generator that gets my words out of the mic and into people's radios. The original of that cartoon hangs on my office wall — another contribution by this most faithful and artistic listener.

" GOOD EVENING AND WELCOME TO 'ALL THINGS CONSIDERED'.... I'M SUSAN STAMBERG, NOAH ADAMS IS ON ASSIGNMENT TONIGHT."

Between crises, I asked Jim Borgman about his kindness to public radio. Why all the generous contributions and attentions? His answer was sobering and satisfying. "Because you're the lifeline." Then he explained that he listened to our news and public affairs program every evening so that he'd know what was going on in the world, and be able to draw it for publication the next day (or in the small hours of the night — who knows about the work habits of a guy like this?)

I confess that his answer gave me pause. It's one thing to be reporting on world events for the ears of our listeners. It's another thing to know that two of those ears will convert our words into something intended for eyes only. Television, as the world knows, is merely radio with pictures. But what to say about an editorial cartoon that uses radio as the basis for visual information?

This puzzlement nearly gave me lockjaw for several weeks. Here we were, on *All Things Considered*, in a spoken but unseen partnership with one of the nation's best scribblers — a Pulitzer Prize Finalist, for gosh sakes — available in 200 papers nationwide. Satisfying and sobering, indeed.

And it tells you something about how Borgman works. For a funpoker, he takes what he does most seriously. He listens and reads, and keeps himself informed in order to show his readers, in a blink of the eye, what it takes radio and television and newspapers many minutes and columns to convey.

And behind that eye-blink, that scrawl of black marks, is a clear moral vision that discerns the difference between right and wrong, idiocy and sobriety, good intention and sham. He's a husband and a father and that shows in his work. The presence of Lynn, his wife, and Dylan, their son, fuels his drawing of a Third World child, its stomach so distended by malnutrition that it rumbles loudly over an empty food bowl, while over in the corner, Ronald Reagan, in infantry gear, presses his ear to the ground and says, "Listen! Just as I suspected! Communist tanks."

Lynn and Dylan are there, too, behind the pen that draws a pig-tailed girl on a swing — "Meet Jennifer," writes Borgman, "too young to be taught the facts of life. Too sweet to be troubled with the confusion of sex. Too innocent to have her happy world disturbed." Then, in the next box, a puzzled-looking baby, and this caption: "Meet Jennifer's daughter."

He's quite a communicator, this Jim Borgman. Too modest to call himself a Great one, he leaves that adjective to White House occupants and book titles. But you'll likely feel, when you finish leafing through these pages, that the "Great" looks quite smart next to Borgman's name, too.

— Susan Stamberg

Susan Stamberg is co-host of National Public Radio's *All Things Considered*

The President Gets a Hearing Aid:

9/12/83

12/4/84

"UP! I'VE GOT ONE STUDENTLOANBURGER.... ONE FARMPROGRAMBURGER... ONE LEGALSERVICESBURGER.....
ONE REVENUESHARINGBURGER......, AND ONE WEINBERGER!"

2/6/85

"WHEEEEEE! DON'T LET ME INTERRUPT!"

The 20th anniversary of President Kennedy's assassination   11/15/83

14

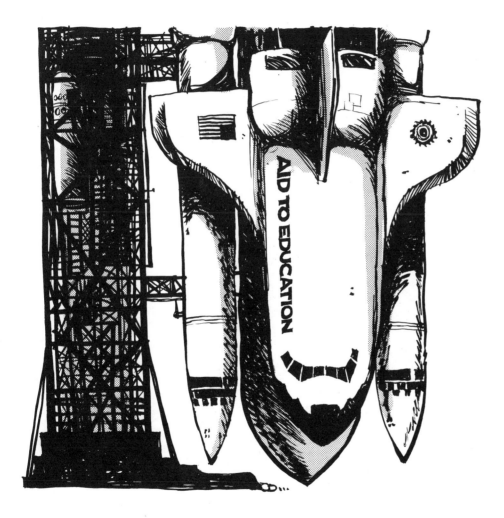

The first private citizen in space will be a teacher.

7/24/85

DEFENSE CONTRACTOR

3/29/85

16

CAP THE KNIFE

4/12/83

12/27/82

"…. YES, BUT AT LEAST I'M NOT ENJOYING MYSELF!"

2/1/83

WELCOME TO THE WORLD, BABY!

HAVE FUN, BUT GET A LOT OF REST. BECAUSE A MAN NAMED RONALD REAGAN HAS BIG PLANS FOR YOU!

HE'S SPENDING BILLIONS OF DOLLARS EVERY DAY AND PUTTING IT ON YOUR TAB. THAT'S CALLED DEFICIT SPENDING.

AND HE'S PROMISED NOT TO TAMPER WITH THE SOCIAL SECURITY SYSTEM, SO YOU'LL HAVE TO MAKE LOTS OF MONEY TO PAY MOMMY AND DADDY'S WAY...

WHERE WILL SOCIAL SECURITY BE WHEN YOU NEED IT? ALLLLL GONE!

ONE MORE THING, BABY..... MR. REAGAN WANTS TO KNOW WHY YOU HAVE NO FAITH IN THE FUTURE?

7/13/84

12/13/83

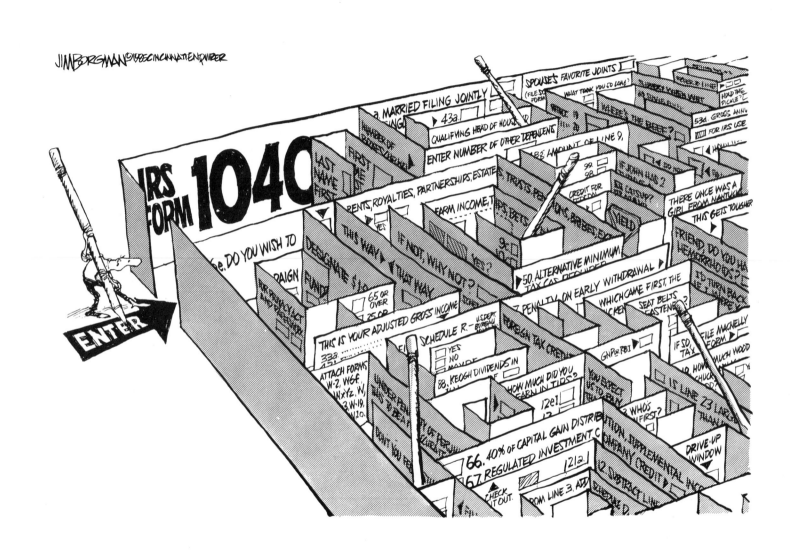

2/12/85

4/15/85

"SIMPLIFICATION! NOW THAT'S SOMETHING I'M GOOD AT!"

5/30/85

24

6/5/85

"HONEY, DO WE WISH TO DESIGNATE $1 OF OUR TAXES FOR THE UNEMPLOYED-TAX-LAWYERS-AND-ACCOUNTANTS FUND, YES OR NO?"

8/15/84

JIMBORGMAN©1985CINCINNATIENQUIRER

COMPLAINTS

2/27/85

27

BERNHARD HUGO STOCKMAN

Four thugs accost Bernhard Goetz in a New York City subway; he shoots them, fueling the nation's fantasies about vigilantism.

2/18/85

"HAVEN'T YOU HEARD?.... THEY SAY HE'S ATTRACTED TO RED..."

4/2/85

29

7/30/85

1/8/85

8/6/85

8/2/85

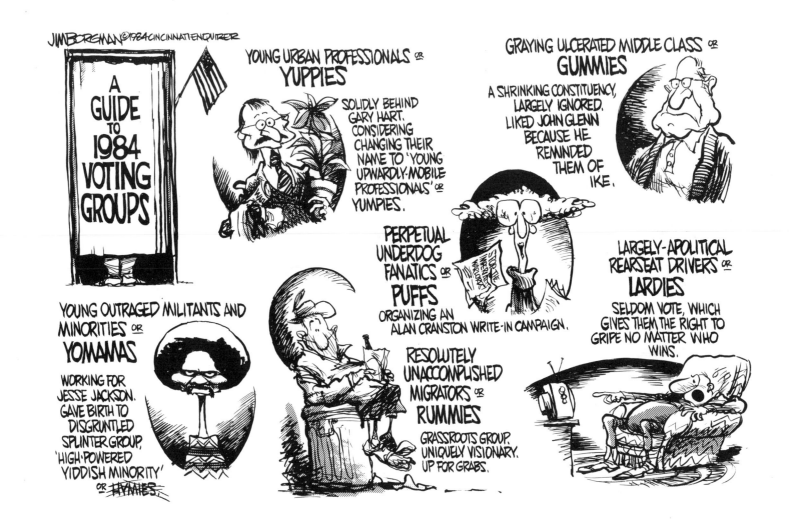

JIM BORGMAN ©1984 CINCINNATI ENQUIRER

A GUIDE TO 1984 VOTING GROUPS

YOUNG URBAN PROFESSIONALS OR **YUPPIES**

SOLIDLY BEHIND GARY HART. CONSIDERING CHANGING THEIR NAME TO 'YOUNG UPWARDLY-MOBILE PROFESSIONALS' OR YUMPIES.

GRAYING ULCERATED MIDDLE CLASS OR **GUMMIES**

A SHRINKING CONSTITUENCY, LARGELY IGNORED. LIKED JOHN GLENN BECAUSE HE REMINDED THEM OF IKE.

PERPETUAL UNDERDOG FANATICS OR **PUFFS**

ORGANIZING AN ALAN CRANSTON WRITE-IN CAMPAIGN.

LARGELY-APOLITICAL REARSEAT DRIVERS OR **LARDIES**

SELDOM VOTE, WHICH GIVES THEM THE RIGHT TO GRIPE NO MATTER WHO WINS.

YOUNG OUTRAGED MILITANTS AND MINORITIES OR **YOMAMAS**

WORKING FOR JESSE JACKSON. GAVE BIRTH TO DISGRUNTLED SPLINTER GROUP, 'HIGH-POWERED YIDDISH MINORITY' OR ~~HYMIES~~.

RESOLUTELY UNACCOMPLISHED MIGRATORS OR **RUMMIES**

GRASSROOTS GROUP. UNIQUELY VISIONARY. UP FOR GRABS.

4/10/84

36

2/26/84

Gary Hart wins decisively in the New England Democratic primaries.

3/7/84

3/16/84

"LOOK! IT'S GARY HART! .... IT'S OK, GARY, WE'RE JUST CIVILIANS!"

In response to the Soviet downing of a civilian airliner, candidate Hart proposes peeking in the windows before shooting in the future.

3/15/84

3/20/84

2/27/84

6/28/84

THE AMERICAN QUILT

7/19/84

11/7/83

"NOW, SOME WILL UNDOUBTEDLY CHOOSE TO SEE THIS AS SUBMITTING TO PRESSURE..."

7/9/84

"WE INTERRUPT THIS PROGRAM FOR ANOTHER BULLETIN ON THE ECONOMIC RECOVERY..."

7/16/84

JIM BORGMAN CINCINNATI ENQUIRER ©84 IN SAN FRANCISCO

7/20/84

48

10/9/84

"TESTING...TESTING.....THERE ONCE WAS A GIRL FROM NANTUCKET..."

Into an open mic, Reagan jokes, "I'm pleased to announce we've just signed legislation outlawing Russia forever. We begin bombing in five minutes."

8/20/84

"... AND I'VE GOT A MILLION OF 'EM!"

8/16/84

JIM BORGMAN ©1983 CINCINNATI ENQUIRER

3/21/84

"YOU CALLED THE GHOSTBUSTERS?"

7/31/84

"DON'T ASK ME – I'M ONLY THE PIANO PLAYER!"

4/5/84

10/18/84

The Teflon President

STOP ERA

GOP

REPUBLICAN WOMEN AGAINST ERA

I CAN BAKE A BLUEBERRY MUFFIN

The Tupperware Party

8/23/84

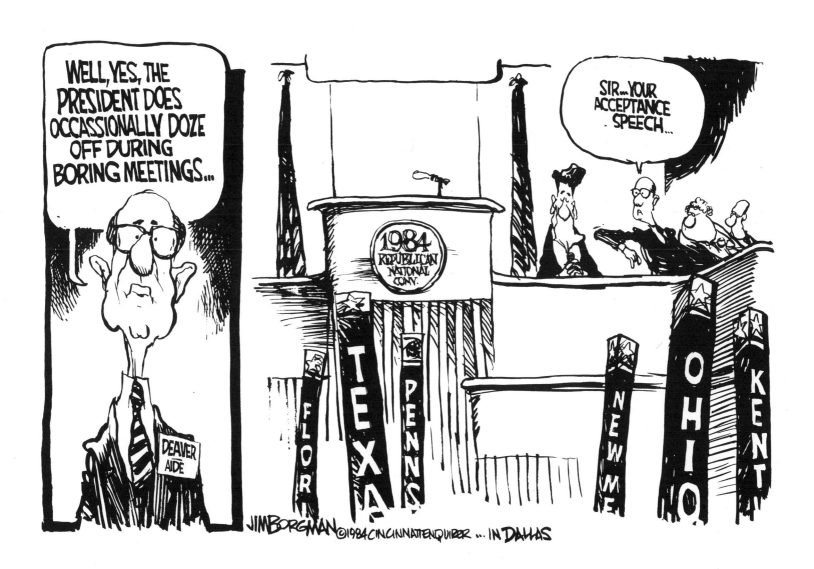

8/24/84

9/24/84

ON RAISING TAXES

10/31/84

THE CARTOONIST SITS THE PRESIDENT DOWN:

I'M A CARTOONIST, MR. PRESIDENT, AND DON'T BOTHER CALLING SECURITY, SIR.... I'VE ERASED THEM.

MR. PRESIDENT, WE HAVE TO HAVE A LITTLE TALK. NOW JUST SIT THERE AND LISTEN A MINUTE.

SIR, IN A FEW DAYS YOU ARE GOING TO BE RE-ELECTED. IF THAT'S WHAT MOST OF THE PEOPLE WANT, OK.

BUT A WHOLE LOT OF US WON'T BE VOTING FOR YOU, AND YOU'LL BE OUR PRESIDENT, TOO..... SO LISTEN UP...

WE DON'T LIKE THE WAY YOU'RE LEAVING HARD-WON CIVIL RIGHTS PROGRESS TO WITHER ON THE VINE. START BEING MORE ACTIVELY SUPPORTIVE.

SIT DOWN, SIR. WHILE YOU'RE AT IT, WHY DON'T YOU JOIN THE 20TH CENTURY IN YOUR ATTITUDE TOWARD WOMEN'S RIGHTS....

QUIT YOUR ENVIRONMENTAL POSTURING AND START WORKING— HARD— TO UNDO YOUR DAMAGE. QUIT LEAVING THE BILLS FOR YOUR DEFENSE BUILDUP ON OUR CHILDREN'S DOORSTEPS. OH, AND SPARE US THE DUMB JOKES, HUH?

I DRAW YOUR HAIR GRAY. NOW, PICK UP THAT PHONE AND FIRE CASEY...

10/30/84

"ENCORE! ENCORE!"

Reagan wins by a landside.

11/7/84

11/12/84

"NO QUESTIONS, PLEASE..... THIS IS JUST A PHOTO•OP."

1/17/85.

Meet Jennifer.

She's just fourteen.

Too young to be taught about the facts of life.
Too sweet to be troubled with the confusion of sex.
Too innocent to have her happy world disturbed.

Meet Jennifer's daughter.

5/3/85

66

3/26/84

4/3/84

6/23/85

JIMBORGMAN ©1983 CINCINNATI ENQUIRER

PRAVDA

ANDROPOV DOWN 115 DAYS WITH SNIFFLES

BREZHNEV STILL UNDER THE WEATHER

STALIN CAN'T SHAKE BUG

LENIN 'NOT HIMSELF LATELY'

11/10/83

"..... AND THIS, MR. SECRETARY, IS OUR PROCUREMENT STAFF...... COMMANDER CURLY, ADMIRAL LARRY AND GENERAL MOE."

3/11/85

2/7/84

6/22/83

"THE GOOD NEWS IS, THEY THINK THEY'VE FOUND JOSEF MENGELE'S GRAVE ..... THE BAD NEWS IS, CHANCELLOR KOHL HAS ASKED IF YOU'LL LAY A WREATH THERE."

A Nazi war criminal's remains are found.

6/16/85

7/14/85

5/19/85

The bomb turns 40.

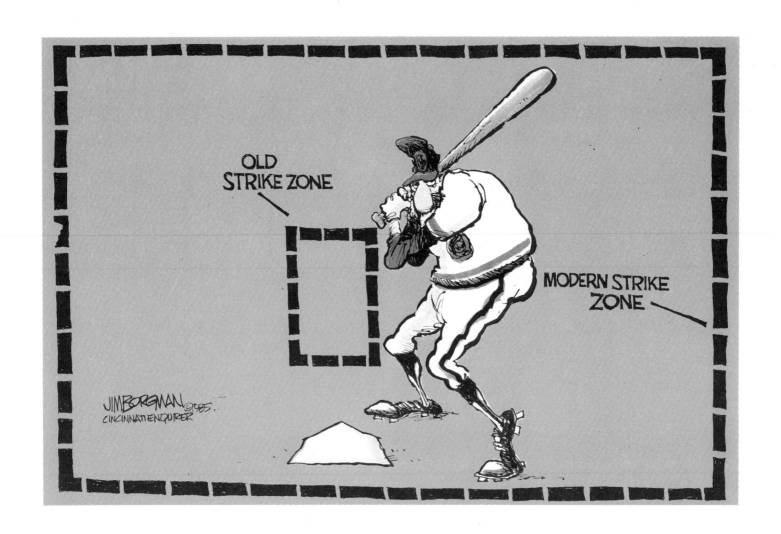

8/11/85

"DON'T YOU SEE? THEY WERE GROOVY AND BOSS, HIP BUT KIND OF BOFFO....."

2/6/84

" I HAVE NOT BEEN SEEINK SUCH COLD AND GLOOMY PLACES SINCE MY OLD KGB DAYS!"

11/22/82

CINCINNATIENQUIRER
JIM BORGMAN ©1983

TECHNOLOGY

LEECHES

5/3/83

FINGERPRINT FOUND ON THE GUN OF ALI AGCA

The assassination attempt on the Pope is traced back to the Soviets.

1/10/83

Andropov dies after 15 months in office.

2/14/84

Soviets boycott the Los Angeles Olympics.

5/10/84

OLYMPIC HAMMER-THROW

5/9/84

JIM BORGMAN ©1983 CINCINNATI ENQUIRER

A STRATEGY FOR THE 1990s

THEY BUILD A MISSILE.

WE BUILD A BEAM THAT SHOOTS DOWN THEIR MISSILE.

THEY BUILD A SHIELD THAT CUTS OFF OUR BEAM.

WE BUILD A TANK THAT DESTROYS THEIR SHIELD.

THEY BUILD A GUN THAT BLOWS UP OUR TANK.

WE GET A BIG CLUB AND ATTACK THEIR GUNNER.

THEY THROW ROCKS AT THE WHITE HOUSE WINDOWS.

WE CALL 'HEADS', DECLARE VICTORY IN WWIII.

Star Wars

3/29/83

A LONG TIME AGO, IN AN ADMINISTRATION FAR, FAR AWAY....

1/9/85

1/15/85

4/1/85

Chernenko dies after one year in office.

"WELL, WELL, WELL ... GET A LOAD OF MISTER CHARISMA OVER HERE ......"

12/30/84

JIMBORGMAN©1983CINCINNATIENQUIRER

9/6/83

94

5/6/85

"NO KIDDING? I'M A MAN OF PEACE MYSELF!"

2/22/83

UNDISPUTED ARMS-WRESTLING CHAMPION

10/16/84

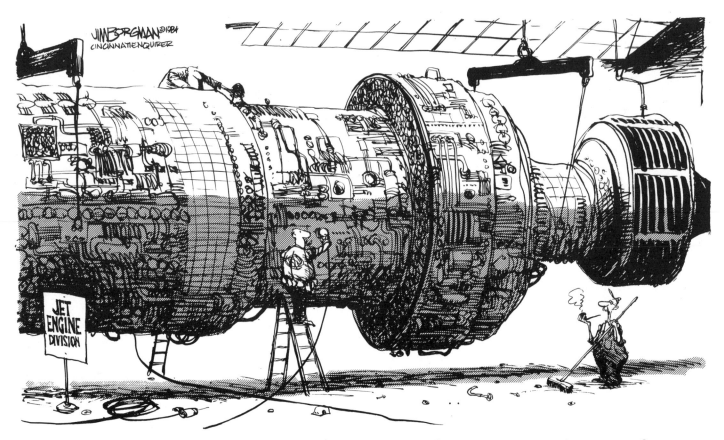

"YEP, I PICK UP ALL THESE LITTLE DOOHICKIES YOU FELLAS DROP... MADE FOURTEEN MILLION BUCKS LAST YEAR IN THE SPARE PARTS BUSINESS."

10/15/84

"I CAN'T AFFORD AN ATTORNEY, YOUR HONOR ..... I ONLY HAVE THESE THIRTY PIECES OF SILVER."

A family of spies betrays Navy secrets.

6/7/85

"I'LL PROBABLY KICK MYSELF LATER FOR SAYING THIS, BUT...."

The President has a penchant for misstatements.

2/3/83

"....OK, THEN, IT'S NOT EVEN REALLY A GET-ACQUAINTED MEETING ...... WE'LL JUST HAVE YOU BUMP INTO EACH OTHER AT A SHOPPING MALL ... "

7/9/85

" IT MAKES EVERYTHING SEEM MUCH MORE PALATABLE ! "

6/13/85

10/9/83

2/8/84

" SO YOU SEE, YOUR FEARS ARE UNWARRANTED! THE TECHNOLOGY IN A NUCLEAR POWER PLANT IS ABSOLUTELY FOOLPROOF! "

3/16/83

"THESE CHASE SCENES WERE A LOT MORE EXCITING BEFORE JAMES WATT GOT HERE..."

8/11/83

108

" I'M MELTING! I'M MELTING! OOOH, MY BEAUTIFUL WASTE DUMPS! MY SHREDDED RECORDS! MY CONTEMPT CHARGES! GONE!... GONE!... "

3/14/83

THE RETURN OF THE PRODIGAL SON

3/22/83

"WHY, YOU MUST BE NEW IN TOWN, AND SO HANDSOME, TOO! WE'LL TREAT YOU REAL FINE, HONEY....
NOW, WHAT CORPORATION DID YOU SAY YOU'RE WITH?"

5/10/83

I'M THE EPA.
BACK IN '70 I WAS INTO EARTH DAY...

AND IN '72 I WAS INTO SAVING
THE BABY SEALS...

BY '75 I WAS INTO GREENPEACE
AND SAVING THE WHALES...

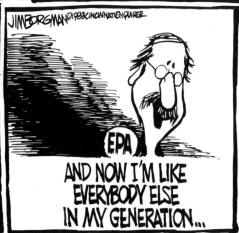

JIM BORGMAN ©1983 CINCINNATI ENQUIRER

AND IN '78 I WAS INTO
STOPPING ACID RAIN.

AND NOW I'M LIKE
EVERYBODY ELSE
IN MY GENERATION...

........I'M INTO INDUSTRY.

3/9/83

8/19/85

7/12/83

6/1/83

10/27/82

FIRST, WE LAUNCH AN ALL-OUT ATTACK ON THE FREEDOM OF INFORMATION ACT...

THEN WE SEAL ALL LEAKS IN THE GOVERNMENT AND MAKE EMPLOYEES TAKE LIE —

DETECTOR TESTS, AND OATHS OF SECRECY COVERING FUTURE WRITING.

...WE'LL TELL YOU WHAT WE THINK YOU SHOULD KNOW ABOUT THINGS LIKE GRENADA.

WE'LL ALL BE A LOT BETTER OFF.

HAVE A NICE DAY!

11/30/83

"OK, IT'S BACK TO THERAPY FOR YOU, SMAGARINSKY!"

Cocaine in professional sports

11/20/84

"OH GREAT! THIS'LL PROBABLY HAVE ALL THE ANTI-BOXING FANATICS OUT HOWLING AGAIN....."

10/8/84

119

The Subway Vigilante is acclaimed a hero in New York City.

1/7/85

120

The Philadelphia police bomb the MOVE cult, destroying an entire city block.   3/22/85

3/12/85

"IT'S THEM, BERNARD! IT'S THE BETAMAX PATROL AND THEY'RE COMING THIS WAY! HURRY — FLUSH <u>BEN-HUR</u> DOWN THE TOILET!"

1/24/83

"TOMMY LOPOWSKI, OELWEIN, IOWA.... NAUGHTY-OR-NICE SEARCH?... ONE MOMENT, BOSS, LET ME CALL THAT UP..."

12/7/84

A few moments of your time could change his life forever.

©1984 JIM BORGMAN
CINCINNATI ENQUIRER

That's right. It doesn't take long to introduce a kid to alcohol. Or give him his first joint. Or touch a little girl where you shouldn't. Or take out your frustrations on a little kid's body.

It doesn't take much time on your part. But he'll never be the same.

Kids. Keep your lousy hands off 'em.

5/23/84

"EVER SINCE WATCHING TWO STRAIGHT WEEKS OF THE OLYMPICS, BERNIE ONLY MOVES IN SUPER-SLO-MOTION."

8/14/84

A second baseball strike in four years

8/8/85

"WELL, YOU LEARN SOMETHING NEW EVERY DAY! I ALWAYS THOUGHT IT WAS JUST THE SHOES!"

11/14/83

TRADE
TALKS

JIM BORGMAN
©85 CINCINNATI ENQUIRER

4/4/85

INDIRA GANDHI

©1984 CINCINNATI ENQUIRER
JIM BORGMAN

Indira Gandhi is assassinated, touching off sectarian violence.

11/5/84

NONVIOLENCE

SIKHS
HINDUS
MUSLIMS

JIMBORGMAN
©1984 CINCINNATI ENQUIRER

11/8/84

The World Court condemns U.S. mining of Nicaraguan harbors.

4/12/84

The U.S. invades Grenada.

10/31/83

THE BOY WHO CRIED "CRISIS!"

5/24/84

8/17/83

"I'LL NEVER CUT SOCIAL SECURITY.... I MEAN, OF COURSE I'LL CUT SOCIAL SECURITY.... THEN I'LL GO VISIT A GERMAN CEMETERY.... I MEAN, A CONCENTRATION CAMP.... NOW ON THE SUBJECT OF NICARAGUA......"

4/22/85

"MR. PRESIDENT?..... IS SOMETHING WRONG, SIR?..... MR. PRESIDENT?..... "

Reagan agrees to visit a German cemetery at Bitburg where Nazi SS troops are buried.   5/2/85

HORN OF AFRICA

Famine in Ethiopia

11/1/84

11/13/84

141

Live Aid

4/29/85

5/27/85

JIM BORGMAN ©1985 CINCINNATI ENQUIRER

WWII

40 YEARS AGO

VIETNAM

10 YEARS AGO

WATCH THIS SPACE

NICARAGUA

4/29/85

" I'VE JUST SIGNED LEGISLATION OUTLAWING NICARAGUA FOREVER. WE BEGIN BOMBING IN FIVE MINUTES .... WHY IS EVERYONE SMILING? "

11/26/84

The Reagan administration establishes station Radio Marti, broadcast to Cuba to encourage dissidence.

5/23/85

"AS YOU CAN SEE FROM THIS NEXT SLIDE, GENTLEMEN, CATHOLIC BISHOPS HAVE BEEN ASSOCIATING WITH KNOWN DOVES FROM THE BEGINNING..."

Catholic bishops write a Pastoral Letter on world peace.

11/25/82

JIM BORGMAN ©1985 CINCINNATI ENQUIRER

A BRIEF INTERMISSION FROM THE CONSTRUCTIVE ENGAGEMENT TALKS

8/20/85

World oil glut

3/2/83

"WELL, SO MUCH FOR THE GAS GLUT."

6/23/83

11/8/83

"NOW, I'M SURE WE CAN ALL FIND SOME COMMON GROUND BETWEEN US.,,,, ER.,,.. LET ME REPHRASE THAT.,,"

Jordan joins the U.S. Mideast peace effort.

4/11/83

Support for the President's strategy in Lebanon erodes.

1/5/84

JIM BORGMAN ©1983 CINCINNATI ENQUIRER

Semper FiASCO

THE DEAD

U.S. POLICY IN LEBANON

Terrorists strike a U.S. peacekeeping base in Lebanon.

11/9/83

"WE WILL NOT CHANGE OUR POSITION VIS·A·VIS TERRORISM..."

The Beirut hijacking

6/26/85

6/28/85

"DON'T WORRY ABOUT A THING, SIR..... WHILE YOU WERE RESTING I ACCEPTED A BUDGET COMPROMISE WITH CONGRESS, APPOINTED YOUR NEW OMB DIRECTOR AND ORDERED A LONG-OVERDUE RETALIATORY STRIKE ON LEBANON ....."

Reagan convalesces after cancer surgery.

7/19/85

GREAT COMMUNICATORS

9/6/85